Contents

What are drugs?

A drug is something that affects your body and the way you feel. People take drugs for all sorts of reasons. Doctors give medicinal drugs to people to make them feel better. But some people take drugs to change how they feel or think.

Drinking alcohol, a legal drug, is how many people relax with friends.

Legal drugs

You have probably taken several drugs during your lifetime. Headache pills and antibiotics are medicinal drugs that help you get better if you are unwell. Tea, coffee and chocolate contain a stimulant drug called caffeine. Tobacco and alcohol are also legal drugs.

Medicines can make people feel better when they are ill.

Illegal drugs

Governments decide which drugs are to be illegal (against the law). Over time, certain drugs have been made illegal because of the dangerous effects they have on the person who has taken them. The danger might be to themselves or to other people as a result of their behaviour on drugs.

Your view

Alcohol and tobacco are drugs because they change how we think and feel. Why do you think most people don't see them as problem drugs? Is it because they are legal, or because they have been used for hundreds of years?

The drugs heroin, opium and morphine are all made from the opium poppy, shown here.

Plants and chemicals

Some drugs, such as cocaine and heroin, come from plants. Others are made in factories from chemicals. Sometimes people use household products, such as glues and aerosols (solvents), as drugs.

Illegal drugs

There are many different types of illegal drug. The ones you are most likely to hear about are amphetamines (or speed), cannabis, cocaine, crack, ecstasy, heroin, LSD (acid) and magic mushrooms. There are also many others that are not as widely used.

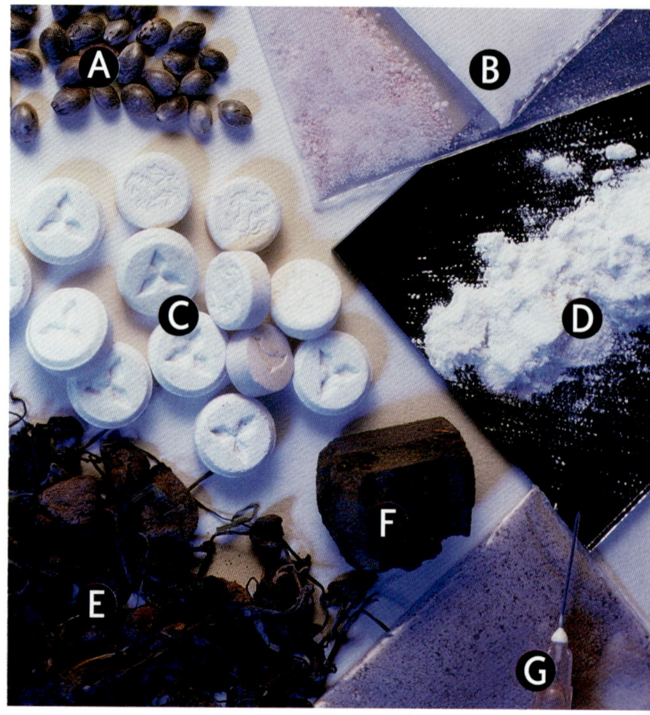

A Cannabis seeds
B Amphetamine
C Ecstasy pills
D Cocaine
E Magic mushrooms
F Cannabis resin
G Needle for injecting heroin

'Hard' and 'soft' drugs

Sometimes illegal drugs are called 'hard' or 'soft', depending on their effect. Hard drugs are generally more dangerous and addictive. Soft drugs are thought of as safer.

What do drugs look like?

Several drugs, including ecstasy, amphetamines and LSD, look like white tablets. Others take the form of a powder, including heroin and cocaine. Cannabis is usually a brown resin, which users smoke in cigarettes or pipes. Magic mushrooms are a type of fungus that people eat.

My experience

"I find the whole drug thing really scary. I know my big brother and his friends have taken drugs. I don't like the way they behave at those times."

Sara, aged 11

Drug	Other names (slang)
amphetamine	speed, wizz, P, base
cannabis	marijuana, grass, dope, weed, pot,
cocaine	coke, snow
crack (crystalline cocaine)	base, rock
ecstasy	E, doves, MDMA, disco biscuits
heroin	smack, gear, skag, junk, H
LSD (lysergic acid)	acid, tabs, trips
magic mushrooms	shrooms, mushies

Your view

One of the main dangers of taking illegal drugs is that, unlike medicinal drugs, they are not carefully checked and labelled. So why do people carry on buying them even though they can't be sure what they have bought?

Where do people buy drugs?

If a drug is illegal, it will not be available to buy in a shop. So a long chain of people has developed who buy illegal drugs from drug producers and sell them on to other people to make money. Drug dealers or 'pushers' are the people who sell illegal drugs on the street or from their home. When someone buys and sells illegal drugs they are breaking the law. If caught, punishments vary from a warning or a fine to a prison sentence (see pages 26-27).

Dealers who sell drugs may be people you know, even your friends.

Drugs and the brain

People take drugs to change how they think or feel. These changes happen because chemicals in the drug affect how the brain works. Everybody reacts slightly differently to drugs.

Injecting drugs is the most dangerous way to take drugs.

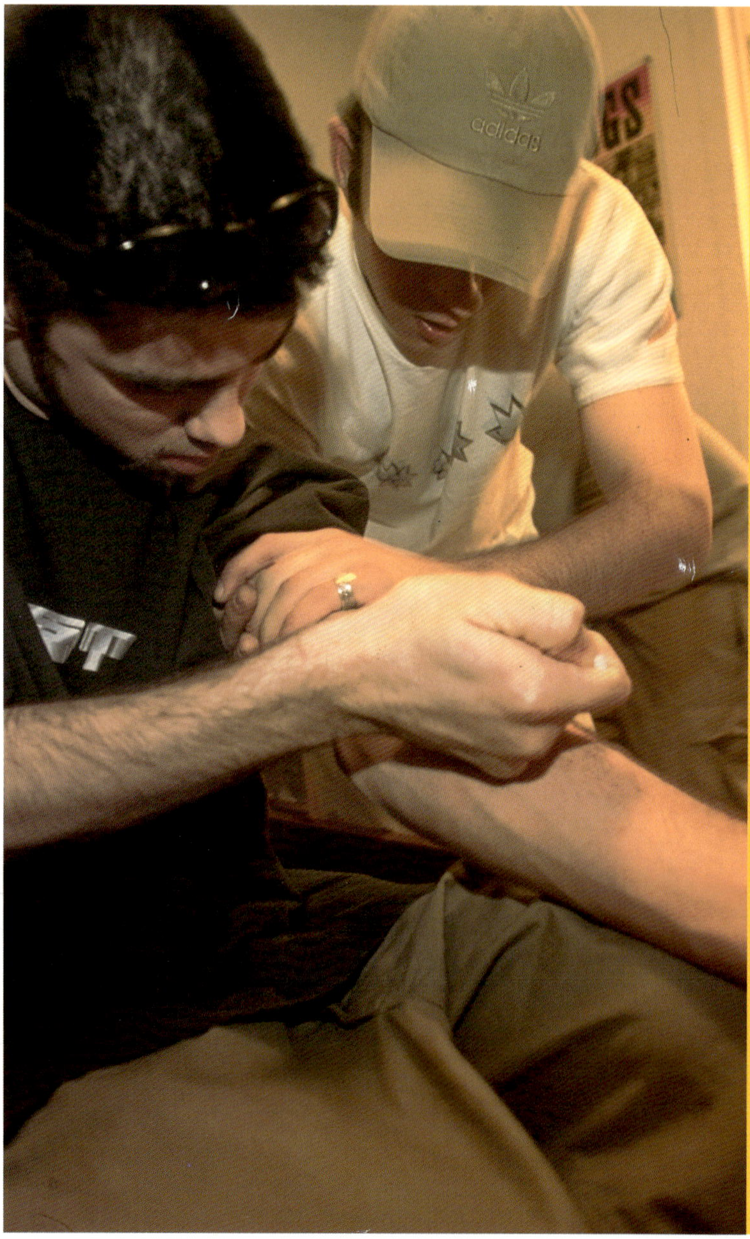

How do drugs reach the brain?

Drugs can be sniffed, smoked, eaten or injected. In each case, the drug then enters the person's bloodstream, which carries the drug to the brain. Smoking or sniffing a drug usually has a very quick effect, which tends to wear off fairly fast. Some drugs are swallowed. It usually takes longer for these drugs to take effect, but the effect lasts longer. Injecting drugs directly into the bloodstream has fast and powerful results that can last a long time.

How do drugs make you feel?

Different drugs produce very different feelings because of the various ways they act on your body. Stimulant drugs, like cocaine, ecstasy and speed, make your brain work faster, causing you to feel more alert and awake.

Depressant drugs, like heroin, have the opposite effect, making people feel calm and more relaxed.

Hallucinogens are drugs that change the way you see and feel things. They include cannabis, LSD and magic mushrooms. Solvents (glues and aerosols) can also have an hallucinogenic effect.

It's your life

For a set amount of time, the drugs discussed on this page can make people feel happy, relaxed, more confident or less anxious. But the effects wear off. However, certain drugs are very addictive. The drugs affect the brain, making the person crave them or come to depend on them to make them feel normal. Tobacco, crack cocaine, alcohol and heroin are amongst the most addictive drugs around — see pages 20-21 for more information. Will you take the risk of becoming addicted to drugs when you are older?

This drug user is unaware of the world around him.

Your view

Why do you think that some people choose to take illegal drugs and others do not? What do you think is the main reason for someone deciding to live a drug-free lifestyle?

Why take drugs?

People have been taking drugs for thousands of years. The ancient Egyptians brewed beer, the native South Americans chewed on the leaves of the coca plant while the ancient Chinese smoked opium.

This man is sniffing, or 'snorting,' a line of the drug, cocaine.

Drug-taking today

Drug-taking has increased over the past 20 years. At the same time, the age at which people first use drugs has got lower. One reason for this is that drugs are cheaper and easier to obtain than in the past. The fact that many drugs are illegal may add to their appeal.

It's your life

Some young people say they take drugs to be like their friends. But friends aren't always good to follow. How much do your friends influence your decisions?

Fun and relaxing

Some young people are curious to see what effects a drug will have on them, and many will find they enjoy it — at least at first. Many people regret ever taking drugs later on in life.

In some places, such as nightclubs, drugs are often easy to buy.

My experience

"When I went travelling I experimented with hash lassi (a cannabis yogurt drink). At first nothing happened, then I just went out of control – nearly jumped off a roof and wandered off into the night. Luckily my boyfriend kept me safe!"

Jayne, aged 21

Stresses and strains

Some people use drugs to help them cope with problems at school, in the family or with friends. Other people may try to use drugs to help them forget about all their problems. Using drugs can then become their greatest problem in life.

Your friends may influence your decision whether to try drugs.

Health risks

Taking illegal drugs may not always be dangerous, but it always carries a risk. While one person may appear undamaged by their drug taking, each person's body reacts differently to drugs so the same may not be true for everyone.

It's your life

Do you want to lose control? If you take a drug you lose some control over how your mind and body works. This can be exciting to some people, but it puts them at risk of accidents or becoming a victim of a violent crime.

Some possible health effects of illegal drug use

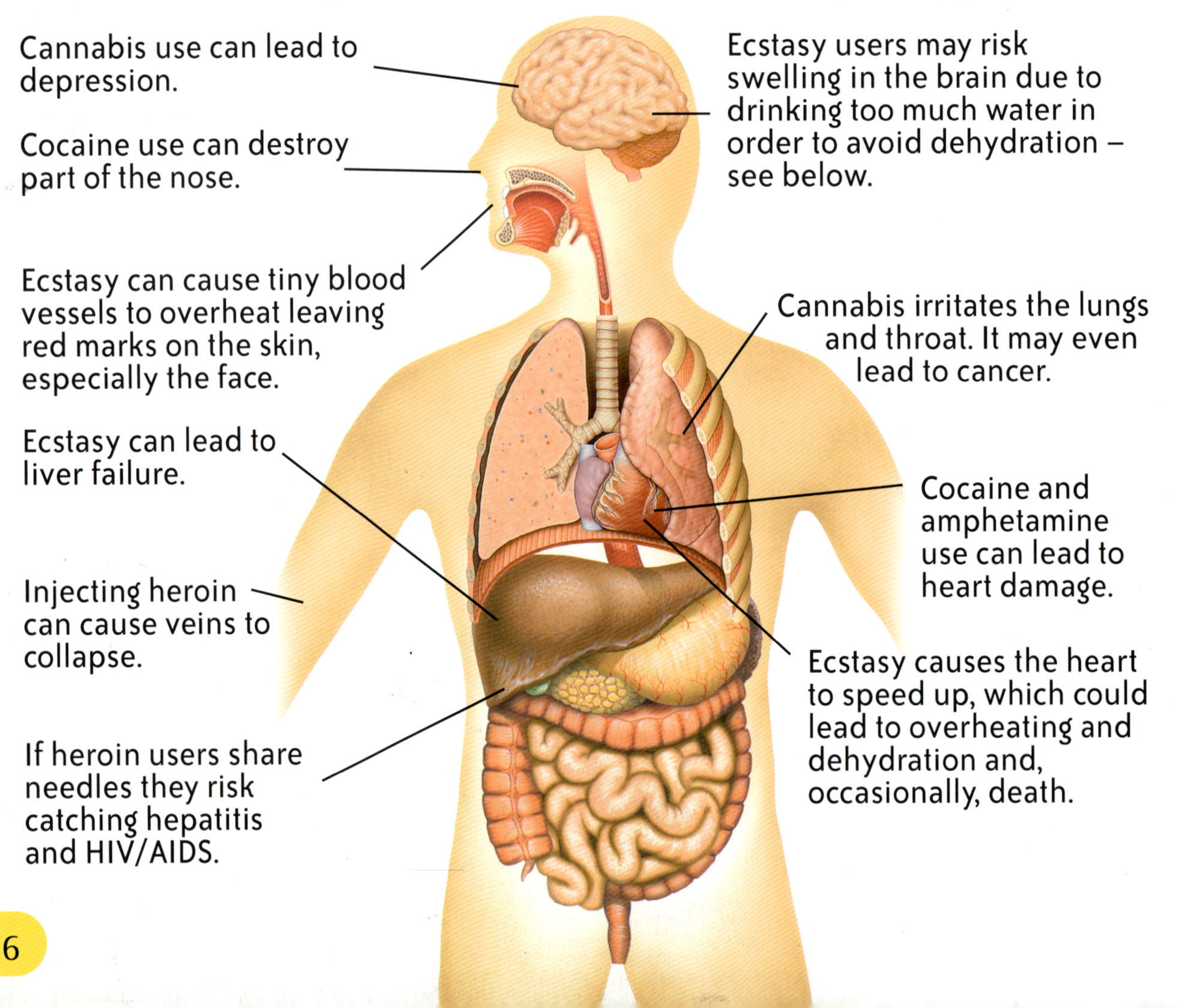

Used, dirty needles are a huge risk for drug takers. Health workers encourage addicts to swap their old needles for clean ones at needle exchanges.

Your view

Do you think the dangers of drug-taking are exaggerated? Far more people die from smoking and drinking alcohol each year than from illegal drug use.

Can drugs kill?

Drugs can be a killer. This is more likely for regular drug users but occasionally first-time users can die from an overdose or reaction. An overdose happens when too much is taken too quickly.

Because each of our bodies is different, people react in different ways to drugs. Mixing drugs with alcohol or other drugs, even ones from the doctor, can lead to dangerous reactions in the body.

In addition, drug dealers sometimes mix drugs with chemicals to make more money, creating a deadly drug by accident.

Certain drugs make people take risks. They might think they can jump safely from a bridge or walk home in the middle of the night. Sadly, some people don't survive these experiences.

Solvent abuse — sniffing glue or aerosols — is the leading cause of drug-related deaths in children and young adults.

Mental health

For many years, scientists and health workers have been looking into the effects that illegal drugs can have on mental health and the mind.

The brain

The human brain is extremely complicated. It is continually reacting to different things around us to control our bodies and work out how we feel about things. Some drugs can make the brain react in unexpected ways.

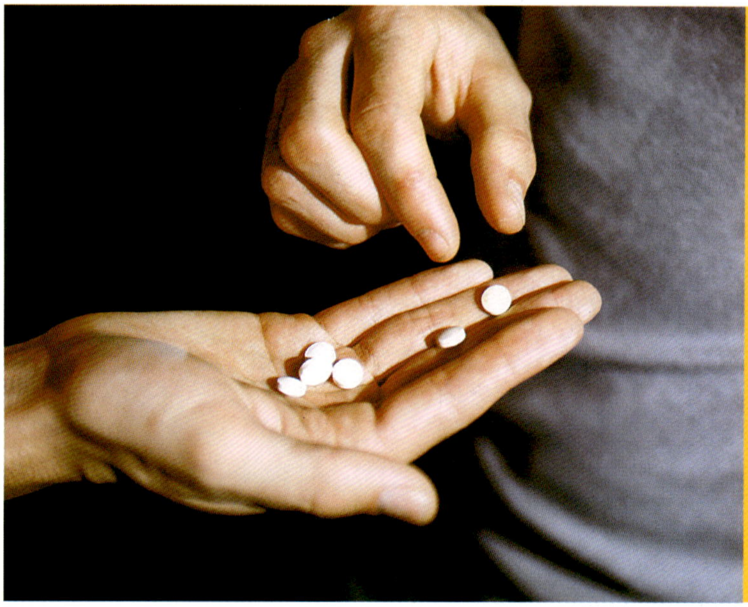

Recent research suggests that people who take ecstasy a lot risk developing mental health problems in the future.

My experience

"My cousin started experimenting with cannabis when he was 15. He wasn't very confident anyway but now he is really depressed and a bit paranoid. We think the cannabis may have caused his problems."

Olivia, aged 14

Bad trip

A 'bad trip' happens when someone has taken an hallucinogenic drug such as LSD. It takes the form of nightmares or bad feelings. Sometimes people get 'flashbacks' where these feelings come back.

Paranoia

Cannabis and other drugs can make users feel anxious and paranoid — worried that people are talking about them or making fun of them. Usually these feelings wear off but sometimes they stay for good.

Feeling high/feeling low

Many drugs, including cocaine and ecstasy, can make people feel 'high' – on top of the world. They may feel in love with everyone, and able to do absolutely anything — sometimes resulting in accidents. After the 'high' feelings have worn off, a user is likely to feel quite low, tired and depressed. Coping with normal life — the good bits and the bad — can be difficult. Research shows that regular drug users are more likely to develop mental health problems than non-drug users.

It's your life

The mood someone is in when they take a drug can affect the way it works on the brain. If someone is happy, it will probably make them happier. If they are feeling down, it will often make them feel worse.

Drug users have to cope with the highs and the lows.

Drug addiction

Sometimes drug use can lead to drug addiction or drug dependence. Drug addiction is when someone's body needs a drug to feel normal. Drug dependence is when someone relies on a drug to cope with normal life, or to have fun.

Actor Robert Downey Junior ended up in prison because of his drug addiction. He has since managed to regain control of his life and is back acting in films.

Your view

Do you think that anyone can become addicted to drugs? Why do some people use addictive drugs even though they probably know the dangers?

Which drugs are addictive?

The most addictive drugs are tobacco, heroin, crack cocaine and alcohol. People can become hooked after only a few uses.

Heroin – highly addictive

People who take heroin usually start with fairly small amounts, but as time passes they have to use more and more to get the same effect. If they don't take the drug, they start to get unpleasant withdrawal symptoms (see pages 24-25). Heroin addiction often leads to crime since the addict will do anything to get money to buy some more heroin.

Heroin is usually injected into the body.

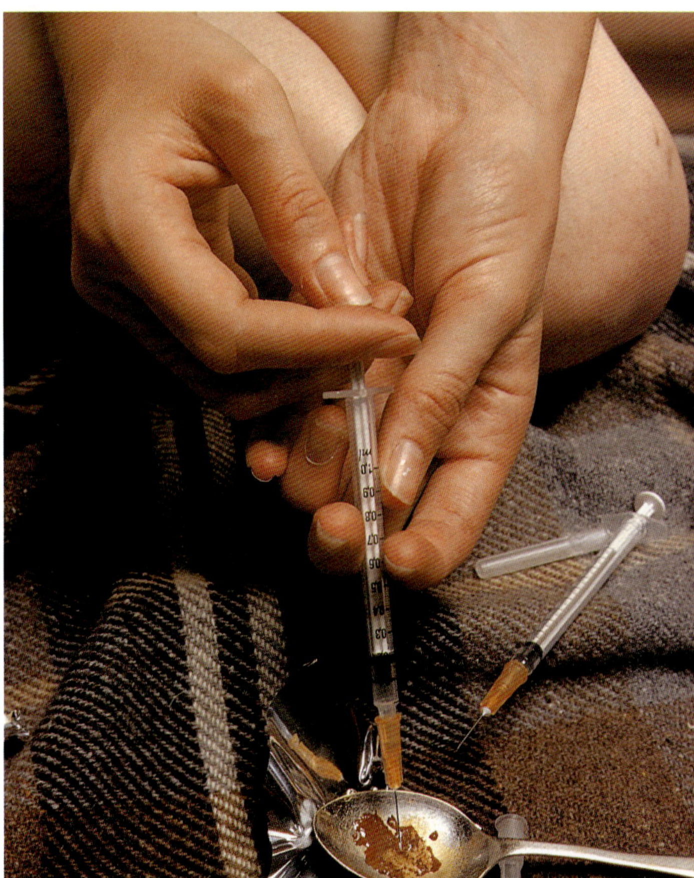

My experience

"I go clubbing most weekends but a couple of years ago I started taking loads of ecstasy. My mate never took it and he always enjoyed himself. He told me to try it drug-free. It's different but it's just as good and I hardly ever do pills now."

Jade, aged 21

Drug dependence

Even drugs that are not addictive, such as ecstasy and cannabis, can still make you dependent on them. This dependence can creep up slowly, without someone realising. Regular users often feel that they need the drug to cope with or even enjoy certain situations. The same can be true for the legal drug, alcohol, and for any other drug. As with drug addiction, the drug user's life can begin to revolve around using the drug. Many regular drug users drop out of school or work and lose interest in pastimes and friends.

Drugs education

At some point you will learn about drugs and their possible dangers. This may be from your parents, teachers, a TV programme or reading this book.

Some people believe that drugs education should start early.

Education in schools

Recently drugs education in schools and youth clubs has focused on giving young people the facts about drugs. Then they will be able to make sensible decisions about whether or not to take them when they are older.

My experience

"We had this woman talking to us about drugs at school recently. She didn't make out that everyone who takes drugs is really bad or anything. She just listened to us."

Jake, aged 15

There are other ways of teaching about drugs. In some schools older pupils talk to younger ones about drugs. This can be particularly helpful because young people are more likely to accept advice from people of a similar age. Sometimes drug addicts are invited to talk to children about the reality of being on drugs and how it has affected them.

A US anti-drug advert compared a drug user's brain with a fried egg. Many experts don't think shock tactics like this work in the end.

Your view

Recent research suggests that when newspapers focus on a few deaths from taking ecstasy, many young drug users switch to cocaine, a more dangerous drug. How do you think the newspapers should behave?

Advertising campaigns

Several governments have tried to use frightening advertising campaigns to stop teenagers from even trying drugs. Research shows that although it may scare them away from drugs at first, they may feel cheated when they realise that some drugs are much less risky than others. In 2003, the UK government launched a new drugs education campaign called 'Talk to Frank' with adverts on television and radio. It is built around a website and chatline that gives advice, information and support.

Confusion

Sometimes the information about drugs can be confusing. Parents may tell you not to take drugs, even if they have done so themselves. There are many organisations that offer advice about drugs. Look on page 43.

Experienced counsellors are just a phone call away.

Giving up

Many people who take drugs decide to stop taking them at some point in their life. This may be because they are worried about their health or the effect that drugs are having on their life or their family.

Courtney Love is one of many people who has struggled to kick a drug habit.

Withdrawal symptoms

If people are addicted to drugs it can be difficult to stop taking them. Because the person's body has become dependent on the drug, stopping the drug can cause unpleasant or even dangerous health problems in the short term. People often need help and support to deal with withdrawal symptoms. These vary according to the type of drug and how quickly the user 'withdraws'. Withdrawing from heroin gives people aches, a runny nose and sweating. Quick withdrawal from certain drugs can cause stomach cramps and rises in blood pressure.

It's your life

Adults can find it hard to give up smoking, even after they have decided to do so. What do you think can help to fight addictions, such as being addicted to drugs?

Support

Addicts who wish to stop taking drugs are supported in many ways. They can talk to trained counsellors about the reasons for their drug use, and attend self-help groups where they can talk to other drug users.

Rehabilitation centres offer addicts a supportive place to live while they are coming off drugs. Several studies show that drug addiction treatment reduces drug use by 40 to 60%. But research also shows that 75% of those that receive treatment at centres will need further help with their drug problem.

Your view

Do you think drug addiction should be treated like any other illness, or does it serve people right for taking drugs?

Art therapy is used by drug rehabilitation centres.

This woman has just picked up some methadone from the pharmacy.

Methadone

Methadone is a drug that has similar effects to those of heroin. Doctors sometimes give it to addicts as it is weaker and less addictive than heroin and can help people give up heroin. It has to be used with care as it is still a dangerous drug.

Drugs and the law

Recreational drugs are illegal, or against the law, in most countries around the world. However the punishments for being caught with drugs or selling them vary from country to country.

There are whole police units devoted to tracking down drug crime.

Legalise cannabis?

There are two strong arguments against making cannabis legal. The 'gateway' argument says that smoking cannabis makes it more likely for someone to come across other drugs. The 'stepping stone' argument says that people will progress from cannabis to drugs like heroin.

Why are drugs illegal?

Over the past 100 years or so, laws have been passed outlawing them. This is because governments have recognised that drugs can be addictive and

Cannabis seed packets. It is legal to grow cannabis in some countries.

My experience

"My aunt's got arthritis, which causes her quite a lot of pain. She told me she smokes a bit of cannabis sometimes as it helps the pain. She's really angry that it's against the law and she has to buy it from a dealer."

Laura, aged 14

also can be bad for people's health.

Punishments

Punishments for selling or using drugs vary from country to country. Usually the most dangerous drugs carry the heaviest punishments, such as a fine or a prison sentence. Remember that even giving an illegal drug to a friend can lead to being prosecuted by the police.

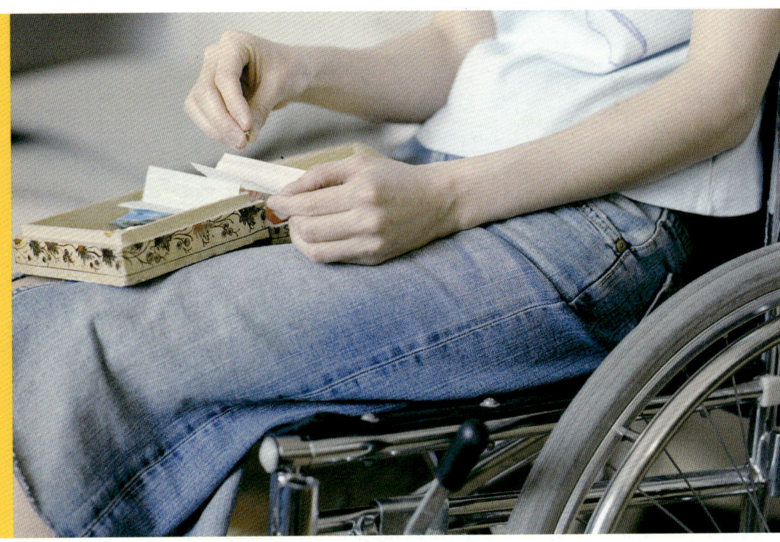

Some people who suffer from arthritis and multiple sclerosis find that cannabis eases their pain.

Changes in the law

Some people think that if drugs were legal they would be less dangerous because scientists would be able to test the drugs and drug users would be able to buy drugs safely without dealing with illegal drug dealers. Other people argue that if drugs were legal more people would use them and the rates of drug addiction would rise.

The cost of drug use

Illegal drugs can be very expensive but drug use has many other, sometimes hidden, costs to the drug user and their family.

The cost of drugs

If someone spends a lot of money buying drugs, they may not have enough to spend on some of the things that make life more enjoyable. Children can suffer because money is short in the family. If people cannot afford to buy drugs they may turn to crimes like burglary to get money to buy their drugs. Drug addicts are likely to drop out of school, college or work, as they are often too tired or unwell to get up in the morning.

My experience

"My nan's flat was burgled by a heroin addict. They caught him and he was sent to prison for a year but my nan is still scared when she is alone."

Aldo, aged 14

Many people turn to crime to get money to buy drugs.

A police haul of illegal drugs in Thailand.

It's your life

If your life is being upset by drug-taking in the family, talk to someone. You could speak to a school counsellor, a trusted adult or phone Childline or another organisation — see page 43.

Police resources

Every year police forces around the world have to spend huge amounts of time and money dealing with illegal drugs and the crimes linked with them. Even then, a vast amount of drug dealing continues unchecked.

Health costs

Millions of pounds are spent helping drug addicts and other drug users, caring for people who have accidents while on drugs and treating those who suffer the ill-effects of drug use. Some people feel that this money could have been better spent elsewhere, treating people who have not risked their health by taking drugs.

Taking drugs can make it hard to get up the next morning.

Drugs in society

Drugs are, or have been, a part of many people's lives for thousands of years. For some young people, experimenting with drugs is part of growing up. Many people stop taking drugs in their twenties.

It's your life

Where do you go with your friends? Who do you choose to spend time with? If you know people who take drugs and places where it goes on, it's up to you to decide if you want to go there. If you'd rather not take drugs, why not go to different places, or choose other friends?

Drugs are much more common in places such as nightclubs.

Drugs and youth culture

In some places, like nightclubs, it is very easy to get hold of drugs and quite a few people there will use them, though of course many will not. Sometimes, if you want to avoid drugs, it is easier to avoid certain places or people and spend time enjoying yourself without using drugs.

Drugs in sport

Sport is something that should be all about health and fitness. Teenagers who are involved in sport are much less likely to start using drugs. However, drugs in sport often hit the headlines. Some sports people use drugs such as steroids to help them perform better. Many of these drugs are not illegal but are banned by a sport because they give the sports person an unfair advantage. Some drugs will build up muscles without exercise, others increase stamina — the ability of the body to keep going.

▲ To combat drugs in sport, sports people are regularly asked to take drugs tests to prove they are drug-free.

Your view

Sports people sometimes forget to go for drugs tests. How should they be treated in sports competitions?

Medicinal drugs

Medicinal drugs are legal drugs that are used to cure and prevent diseases and manage illnesses. There are countless different medicines that are used for a huge variety of reasons.

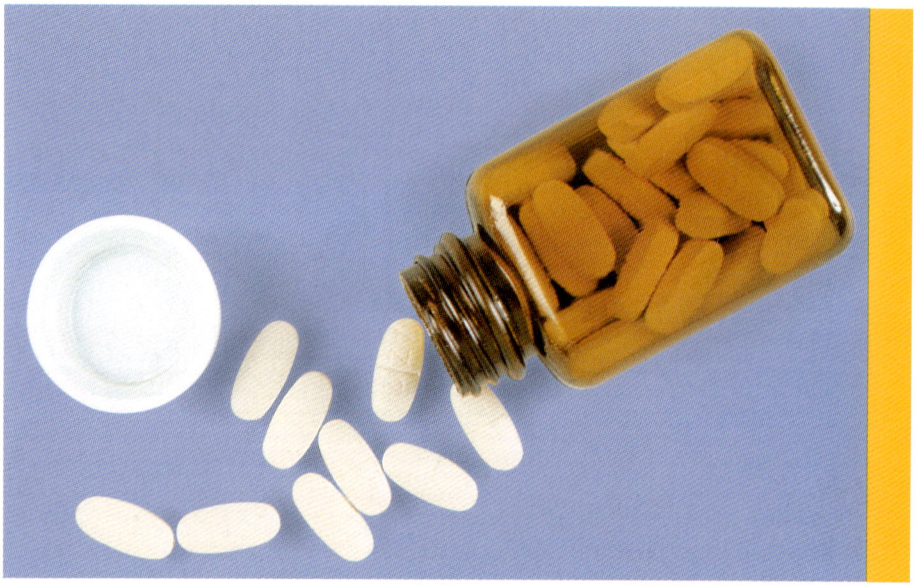

Medicinal drugs are often produced as tablets or pills.

Medicines

Some medicines come as tablets and capsules, others are in powder or liquid form. They may be swallowed, injected, inhaled or even put on the skin as a cream. As with illegal drugs, to have any effect they have to enter the bloodstream.

Medicines are made from all sorts of ingredients, including chemicals, plants and animal extracts. In the past, some of the drugs that are illegal today, such as heroin, were used for pain relief. Morphine, which is made from the opium poppy, is still used as a painkiller.

Your view

When a new medicine is invented it has to be tested to make sure it is safe. Often the drug is tested on animals, before people use them. What do you think about this way of testing medicines?

This man is handing in a prescription to a pharmacy in Africa. Some medicines are only available on prescription after you have visited a doctor.

What are they used for?

Medicines are used to ease pain, prevent and cure diseases, treat conditions such as asthma, put patients to sleep during surgery and help mental illnesses, such as depression. Over the years medicinal drugs have saved and improved the lives of millions of people worldwide.

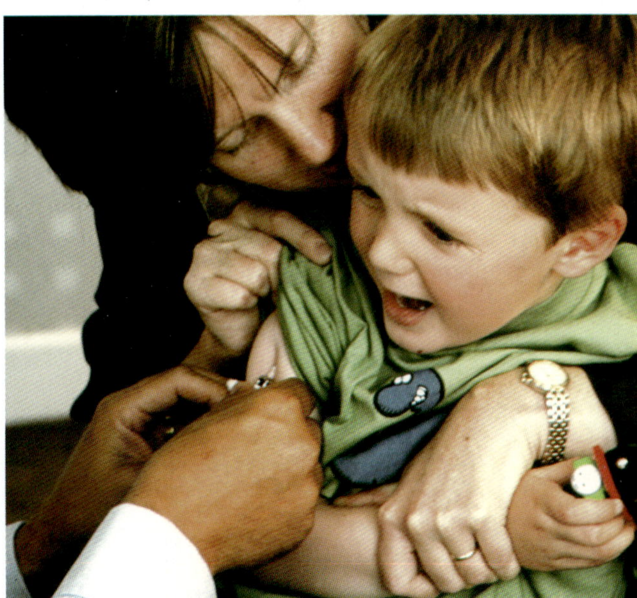

Vaccination drugs have saved thousands of lives.

My experience

"My brother had meningitis when he was a baby. The doctors gave him lots of antibiotics to cure him. Without them he would have died."

Amy, aged 12

The downsides

Medicines help millions of people every year but they can be as dangerous as illegal drugs.

▲ Sometimes people find counselling is more helpful than medicinal drugs.

Side effects

Many medicines have 'side effects'. A side effect is an unwanted effect from taking a drug, maybe a headache or sickness. That is one reason why a doctor will always check whether you are taking any other drugs before giving you a drug to help with an illness or condition.

Overdose

Some medicines are very dangerous if we take too much of them. This is known as an overdose. Even common painkillers, such as paracetamol, can be dangerous. It is important to read the label and follow the instructions carefully.

Your experience

"After my dad died, Mum used pills to help her sleep, but she came to depend on them. It took her ages to get off them and she says she'd never take them again."

Pete, aged 15

Addiction

Sometimes medicinal drugs are addictive. Patients should not be given certain sleeping pills or tranquillisers for more than a

Alison Lapper was born disabled as a result of the drug thalidomide. She is now a successful artist.

Your view

Is it fair that life-saving drugs can be so expensive that they are not necessarily given to people who would benefit from them?

few days at a time because it is easy to get hooked on them. It can be just as easy to become addicted to legal drugs as to illegal ones.

Poor testing

Medicinal drugs usually go through a thorough testing process before they are used. Occasionally the testing is not done well enough. In the late 1950s and early 1960s, doctors gave some pregnant mothers a drug called thalidomide for morning sickness. The drug damaged many unborn children, leaving them disabled. It is now used to treat some cancers.

Expensive drugs

Medicinal drugs take millions of pounds to develop. Sometimes ill people cannot afford the drug.

South Africa has a huge problem with the disease HIV/AIDS. The drugs needed to treat it were very expensive. However, protestors won the right to buy the anti-HIV drugs at lower prices.

South African protestors demanded the right to buy HIV/AIDS drugs at a fair price.

Alternative treatments

Alternative (or complementary) medicines are treatments that fall outside modern medicine.

Acupuncture has been used in China for thousands of years.

What are they?

There are many different alternative medicines. Herbal medicines are made from plants and have been used for thousands of years worldwide. Homeopathy uses tiny amounts of plant extracts to treat a wide range of diseases and other conditions. Some therapies don't even use pills or tablets; acupuncture, for example, uses needles placed into particular parts of a patient's body to ease pain and cure symptoms.

There are thousands of alternative drug treatments available from shops.

Your experience

"I was feeling really stressed and often had backache. I decided to try acupuncture to see if it helped. It was a strange feeling to have needles in my body but it certainly worked for me."

Tina, aged 19

Are they safe? Do they work?

Many doctors and scientists are against alternative medicines. They argue that the treatments often only work because the patients believe they will work. However plants are the base of many modern medicines as well as traditional herbal medicines so perhaps they should work equally well. Much research continues into this fascinating area of healing and people continue to argue whether they work.

It's your life

Some people prefer to live their lives drug-free as much as possible, by eating well and taking plenty of exercise.

Alternative medicines are usually made from plant and animal extracts.

New drugs

Across the world people are researching new drugs to help cure illnesses or to give pleasure.

Here, Alex Krassenberg poses in his business called 'Dr. Paddo, The Natural Drug Store' in the Netherlands. Krassenberg's business offers magic mushrooms, herbal ecstasy, and at least 600 other recreational drugs for sale.

New recreational drugs

Sometimes a new drug will become popular. The drug ecstasy was developed by a chemist a hundred years ago to treat an illness. Then, in the 1970s and 80s, people began to use it for pleasure. Young people discovered it gave them the energy to dance all night.

Another drug that has become popular in nightclubs is methedrone (also known as miaow miaow or M-Cat). Originally developed as a plant food, it has similar effects to ecstasy. Several countries have already banned it as it has been linked to some deaths.

This pictures shows MRSA, an infection that is resistant to common antibiotics.

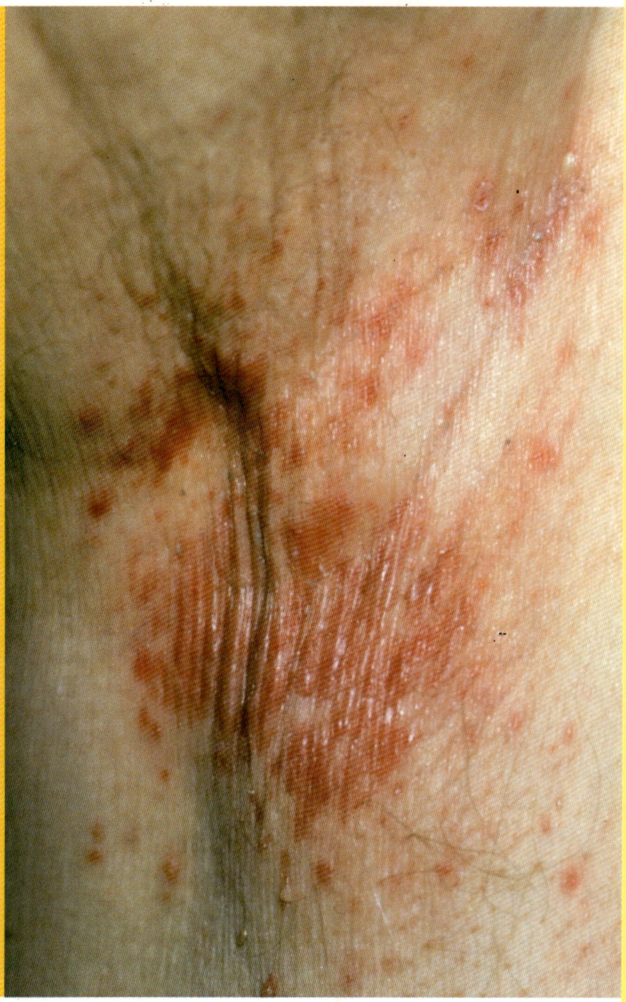

A final warning

All drugs can have side effects whether they are legal, illegal or herbal. Always take care when taking drugs.

New medicines

Drugs companies are constantly developing new medicinal drugs. Some will help people control their weight, others will help to cure cancer, depression or other problems. Sometimes a new disease emerges, such as HIV/AIDS, and scientists have to develop new medicines to treat it.

Unfortunately, some medicines are starting to lose their powers to cure. Antibiotics, which treat bacterial infections, have been overused. This has caused certain bacteria to change so that antibiotics no longer work on them. If doctors and patients are not more careful in the future, antibiotics may stop working.

It's your life

Just as your body will usually recover from illness without using medicinal drugs, so there are many ways to have fun without using illegal drugs.

Drugs and your life

At some point in your life you will find yourself in a situation where illegal drugs are available. It may have already happened. It's up to you to decide what you will do at that point.

Sports and other hobbies are fun ways to spend time with friends.

Pressure

When you are growing up there can be pressure from friends and even members of your family to try new things. Here are some tips on how to cope:

1. Rehearse what you will say.
2. Avoid the places where you are likely to be offered drugs.
3. Spend less time with friends who take drugs and more with friends who don't.

Even more than healthcare, these children need enough food to eat.

Your view

Millions of children die because they don't have clean drinking water, proper housing and enough food to eat. Perhaps some of the money spent on new medicines should be used to tackle poverty? What do you think?

It's your life!

You have to decide whether it is worth risking your health by trying drugs. If you do decide to take drugs, try to be as informed as possible. Check out the websites on page 43 so that you know what to expect. Make sure you are in a safe place with friends if you take drugs.

My experience

"I used to take cocaine at the weekends and smoked cannabis every day. I stopped when one of my mates started doing heroin; I was really worried I was going to go the same way. Now I've got more energy and I'm actually getting somewhere with my life. I've got a job and a girlfriend — things are great."

Zack, aged 18

Most people find happiness without drugs by balancing work and play.

Glossary

Addiction: a habit that is very hard to break.
Antibiotic: a medicine that fights infection.
Bloodstream: the blood circulating within the body.
Dehydrate: to dry out or lose water.
Depression: a sad or low state of mind when people lose interest in everything and feel hopeless.
Drug addict: someone who feels they cannot live without drugs.
Hallucinogenic drug: a drug that makes someone see something that isn't there.
Herbal medicine: alternative medicine made from plants.
HIV/AIDS: HIV is a virus that causes AIDS, Aquired Immune Deficiency Syndrome. This serious medical condition means that the body finds it very difficult to fight off infection.
Illegal: against the law.
Legalise: when a government makes something that was illegal, legal.
Liver failure: when the liver stops working.
Medicinal drugs: legal drugs used to cure or prevent illness or disease.
Meningitis: a dangerous illness that affects the brain.
Mental health: a person's state of mind.
Opium: an addictive drug made from the opium poppy.
Overdose: to take too much of a drug all at once.
Paranoia: a form of mental illness when someone imagines things, often making them very fearful.
Recreational drugs: the name given to drugs that people take for pleasure, such as heroin, ecstasy, cannabis etc.
Rehabilitation: bring someone back to a normal life, especially after they have abused drugs or alcohol.
Solvent abuse: when people use household products, including aerosols, glues and paints, to get feelings similar to being drunk.
Stimulant: something that makes the body speed up and become more alert.
Steroid: a drug that can be used to build up muscles.
Tranquilliser: a drug that calms someone down.
Trip: a strange experience caused by certain drugs, such as LSD.
Withdrawal symptoms: aches, sweating, shaking or other symptoms that occur when someone who takes certain types of drugs stops taking them.

Further information

UNITED KINGDOM

Childline

This is a free, confidential helpline for young people.

www.childline.org.uk/

Drugscope

Use this web address to find the part of the Drug Scope site that is designed for 11-14-year olds. Lots of information about drugs, their effects and the law.

www.drugscope-dworld.org.uk/

PADA (Parents Against Drug Abuse)

Information and support for the families of drug users.

www.pada.org.uk/index.php

Talk to Frank

Advice and information about drugs and other issues. Check the A-Z for how the law relates to each drug listed.

www.talktofrank.com/

The Site

Information about drugs and alcohol.

www.thesite.org/drinkanddrugs

AUSTRALIA

Australian Drug Information Network

Provides links to Internet sites in Australia and elsewhere that have useful information on alcohol and other drugs.

www.adin.com.au/

Children's Youth and Women's Health Service (South Australia)

This link will take you to the child and youth health part of the organisation's website.

www.cyh.com/Default.aspx?p=1

Kids Helpline

Free, confidential helpline for children and young people.

www.kidshelp.com.au/

Note to parents and teachers: Because of the nature of the subject matter and the Internet, these websites may contain material that is inappropriate for some young people. We therefore strongly advise that Internet access is supervised by a responsible adult.

Index